D1713914

COMING

OUT

EVEN

Campbell Reeves

Moore Publishing Company
Durham, North Carolina

Copyright 1973 by Moore Publishing Company,
Durham, North Carolina. All rights reserved. Printed
in the United States of America.

Library of Congress Catalog Card Number: **73-77499**

ISBN 0-87716-043-0

To my husband and
two sons who let
me close doors when
I needed to write

and

To Sam Ragan who
has done so much
for so many of us.

COMING

OUT

EVEN

WALLS

WALLS

Over the brick wall
the roses
short-circuit
the mortar

are you there any more

on which side
can I find the rose-bush
we planted

was it ivory or
red I forget now

who made it grow
who dug it up

fed its roots to pigs
we should have planted
two
roses side by side

I like things to come out even

***

Sun bakes the
brick
intolerable pink

a huge oven
descends

1

the door closes

I am on the wrong side again

***

The walk of
the sun
across the wall

a daily marvel

the sun is supposed
to be a god

gods cannot take back
any
of their gifts

the sun gave me my days

and will not
take them back

although I keep offering

***

Today
a seagull
came skimming over
my side of the wall

a warning of hazards
and coming storms

he did not stay long
on this side

did you see him

***

Once
on a bad day I leaned against it
at a weak spot

it came falling down around us
we were very frightened

those in charge were angry
surprised and
blamed the builders

it was the weather really

nothing has happened since
although I tried leaning harder
and then harder

and once I took a chisel and hammer

one brick fell out
the wall remained

everyone was pleased and felt
secure again

I took the brick and made
one half
of a pair of bookends

***

3

I hear footsteps
on the other side
is it you

or the night watchman

if it is you
what are you wearing

why do you carry a cane

I hear it tapping tapping

*****

A small crack
in the wall
a ray of light

but what kind of light

it may not suit my eyes

let us
mend the crack quickly

before it is discovered

*****

Smoke
from a chimney
drifts
over the wall   forgetful and blue

4

does it come
from your house

do you have a house now

or do you live with eagles

***

Where there are women
there are walls

on them they grow roses
and climbing jasmine

against them they measure
children by loving inches

the walls nurture trees
but the trees and the children

grow look over the parapets
to forest ocean steel and spire

the women stay inside where
all is warm and windless

sometimes they paint
their walls a different color

***

5

My roses like it here
the wall provides
like a good mother shade
and enough shelter

goats graze nearby they
are odorous and cantankerous
but give milk

someone distributes food
and I am able
to carry words and
bars of music in my head forever

***

Someone was careless
and left
the gates wide open for an hour

I stood
in the driveway
staring out with a white face

the tree at
the entrance has grown bigger

a family of lions
lives there now

in the lower branches
they lick at each other and growl

their tails hang down
in gold plumes

their eyes gleam

in the distance I
think I see you hurrying away

they have closed the gates

***

Bees attacked today
from the other
side of the wall

where the queen bee lives
where
they hide the honey

they were confused
one side looks like the other

***

Jericho
what did it require
to topple
the fortress of Jericho

last night you
circled this wall seven times
(I counted)
blowing a silver trumpet
pausing
sometimes to listen

today I inspect the wall
it is sound
and stronger than ever
it did not quiver
at the sound of your trumpet

you have gone away now
but I hear
whistling
somewhere deep in the forest

***

Today
I remember the ocean
tommorrow'
it will be something else

like a fern that grows
tree-size
in a far jungle

or perhaps
a black spider on a coral reef

***

Someone has cut down
the tree
outside the gate

all the lions are falling out

they come towards us
unquiet
irresolute and hungry

you appear
and drive them away how

did you do this

when did you learn to be brave

***

The wall
is growing
like an obsession

does it have roots
with what are they nourished

it grows from the bottom up
a few inches every night
glass remains on top

wounding the feet of birds

if I were to slide
out a brick
at eye level like a loose tooth
would it all collapse

would I find you in the rubble
on the other side

trying to speak to me

***

At midday
expectations   excitement

someone has stolen a ladder

we are all interested
but reluctant
to place it against the wall

a fixation on freedom
demands
action we frenzy leaning
towards each other

wondering
in agitation what to do

it is time for tea
we
postpone any decision

***

They have taken it
the ladder
ropes all the accoutrements
of escape

the road maps compass
and the bow and arrow

everyone saw them do it
in broad daylight
while we were having tea

10

tonight I cry for hours
wondering
why I did not climb the ladder

for tea we had muffins and honey-cake

***

A cannon
fired from the other side
could demolish it

irrevocably immediately

would things then be different
the jasmine would
have nothing to rest upon

the rose
would crawl on its belly
like the snake

bricks
would fall everywhere

we might get hurt all of us

***

If you
were found afterwards
in the rubble on the
other side white-faced
as the
brick-dust
settling around you

11

would you remember me
would I
recognize you I

would need to be
absolutely certain before

I extended my hand

***

If I were
trapped in the debris

and could not be extricated

what would you do then

would you see my arm
in the wreckage
wizened and grey like the
roses
with falling dust

would you hold my hand
pondering
in the tilted shade

or would you cut off my finger
to get
my gold ring

***

12

Daylight
has deafened me
and a dream of somebody
weeping

has made me blind

if light
came into your cave
would your eyes burst

do you trust only mice

***

On the west side
of the wall
it is always morning

in the east afternoon

***

The birds
do not come as often now

flying away
their feet drop blood

***

Tonight
comes the first rain
in a month

the moon is full

what if we should all drown

I dig up the roses
and plant ivy

DISTANCES

BOAT MADE OF GRASS

I set out in a boat made of grass
tied together
with jonquil stems

No fine-wrought ribs or carriage
no canvas
For sail dismembered wing
of a dove
lately fallen

I talked
myself a song shaped like a pyramid,
an ark,
floating in seaweed that
sopped up all echoes.

It is quiet here
remote;
I am pillowed in sand at the bottom
of the ocean, green doomed
seeded with tranquil shells

Vagrant fishes
sleep on their wet dust;
Cat's eyes turn over face downward
blooming blind on the ocean floor

I move unmoving tide-taken to a spillage
of treasure,
ancient coins by the handful;

Each one bears a face
in profile
turning away from me

STILL-LIFE AND SMOKEHOUSE

The cat has brought another bird
an offering
deep-cured in autumn smoke

and dead perhaps an hour.

What to do
Who cares? Not the cat.
She released him only when she yawned.

Even murder becomes a bore;
atrocious in her pride she glows,
furry, butter-sweet and kind.

I have no smoke-house
with a nail for dead birds:
he makes no meal,
his feathers cloak no chieftain
decorate no bonnet
for party or for war;

I house no bats as company for corpses.

This happened once before
when I could hear the water
I held the bird, unconscious in my hand.

His heart turned over once;
the cat yawned
a wing moved   I closed my eyes.

The wind blew tangerine
smokehouse door wide open

I heard the water running in the earth
beneath the roots of trees

And there were eagles in the sky.

PRISMS

Feeling
like Sunday and suddenly
I went inside

The ceiling vaulted above me
windows sliced the dimness

in sandalled feet
and wearing prisms in their robes
like splinters

were all the saints I used to know

The organ woke
rumbled in its golden throat
archaic chords
its fervent declaration flew
against the battlements

18

It shook me like a half-grown tree
of no
particular significance
on Sunday morning
and all the prisms fell

in dislocation at my feet

I bent so low
so lovely low
my branches broke
my heart broke   The organ scolded
and the morning folded me

in equal squares
and left me on the pavement

My eyes   my Sunday eyes
are full of sounds and have no corners

19

THE MAN WHO LOVED OPALS

Nobody told him   but he always knew
how fire had sunk in the opal
like the proving of a new love

into its veins   its arteries
and the cold straw body
in the dry ground

how the opal became everybody
all who live smooth chill and pale
secret and far apart from each other

he stared himself into the opal
it was death in a strange country
flakes of gold drifted

under his heart   shifted
the balance of him entirely
they shattered and broke

drew blood in a few places
it was was ruby-colored
unstable   there was no antidote

his eyes shone strangely
soon he was dotted with small sounds
precious mysterious

they were tribal initiations
no-one could read
translations fell to silence

he lived on and on
inaccessible and shining
pre-occupied with opals

FAMILY ALBUM (New Zealand)

My great-grandmother ran away from England
to marry in New Zealand

and was sorry ever after
He was handsome and a good talker
with a merry eye

She was seventeen
and frail a little flighty
He flourished

like the flax bush
by the river   She had babies
every year some

of them lived   "It
gets so lonely here" she wrote
No-one answered

a country full
of settlers has not time
to answer everything

When old she dreamed
of England in the Spring
Her children

sturdy pioneer stock
straight as kauri never went there
nor wanted to

but at her grave
they planted English lilac.

THE DREDGE AT KAWA-KAWA BAY

(New Zealand)

Eunuch-boat.
Half-ship that sailed nowhere.
Ugly scarecrow. The Dredge.

You could hear it sometimes
Sucking at the channel
If the wind was right, or
If you could bear to look,
To read it like graffiti.

Mornings.
Flax crackling at my bare legs
Caves yawning under the cliffs;
Trees shook flowers out on wet sand,
They fell like unready birds from
A green unfriendly nest.
Morning pools filled slowly
With starfish, sea-anemones.
Mysteries.

The Dredge.
Boat with no name no destination
Thrust a long anchor in my childhood,
More permanent than parents
Seasons, friends.

Its angular arms hold summer tight
And will not let it go.

THE DAPPLED PONIES

When dappled ponies gobbled roses from the hedges
and cobwebs hung spread-eagled from the wires
dew-clotted innocent of victim bait or spider

When morning ran the mists out of the valley
and all the little suns were coming up at once

over the mountain

Then I remember steam from kneeling cattle
rising in mushroom puffs above their heads
the fierce horns the sweet and holy haloes
the heavy beasts all born again

reincarnated saints

Saint Angus and Saint Brahmin a bull
named Gabriel rose like a martyr a wreath
of tenderness around his head

and knelt again sighing

Saints live long but dew is swift in drying

If grace is sought I think about the valley
nurturing its nectarines and honey
the ponies nibbling roses from the hedges

The dappled ponies with their saddles squeaking

THE SPIN OF THE APPLE TREE

The birds die in the sunset
on the hill of the apple tree
I did not hear them sing at the last
their golden hearts
were shredded like cabbages
quickly
in one fast chop

and the thought has written itself now
Something is burning
in this perpendicular of bark
in the winter cold

The apple tree spins and its leaves
fall off
they paste themselves on the sky
on the marbled sides of the upside-down cup
bone china

               bone dry

I beckon you near to read
my fortune
in apples and bones and stuck leaves
and sky

Read quickly
with your rough tongue

            read quickly

If I wait too long the leaves will settle
forever like spiders in a spinster's teacup
sideways tilted hopefully
in the dismal tearoom

the tree will right itself out of my reach
through the cloudy window
and burst with blossoms recycled
all different shades

and the birds reconstituted
will fly out of the fire towards me

It will not do
I have forgotten the language of birds

COUPLE AT THE ART GALLERY

(Quote – "Fulfillment is bondage" – Camus)

You have brought me out of the rain
to this

the slave-girl
fondling her chains

cradling the white garland
closely
against her marble nudity

She is slender
inviolate   blind

I circle the statue
one more time
in my sloppy clothes

The child drags at my hand

as you go on staring
at the slave-girl   at her breasts

at the place where the chains
thicken
and fall into place

PILGRIM IN THE ANDES

Demons have preceded me
to the rain forest

wetting their fingers
to the wind of the endless valley

there is no trail no smoke
no sound of panic yet

my coffin still is growing
in the jungle

We go up into water
are held by water
dew or melted snow or steam

clouds are ruptured
deliver themselves of rain
white and deliberate as madness

and now
the season is arrived
moon-minted acquiescent
our footprints in
the fern are guesses growing fainter

vines curl narrowly the
thinning air
their knotted hands

hold up my coffin tree

TELEGRAMS DON'T REALLY HAPPEN

Rebecca died by telegraph
on yellow paper
early in the morning

I hardly knew it happened

Spring down there
slight and undeserved
(for what is winter but
a damp delusion
a runny nose or two)

Autumn here
boiling in red leaves and
indifference
time between told
by a laggard tide
a cross-eyed noon

I hardly knew it happened
folded up in
disbelief and distance
on yellow paper   early in the morning

THE GOOSE-GIRL

Goose-girl
I must know
I need to tie it together
tight as a noose not
let it run out behind me any more

need to know
where the string ends
the ball in the palm of your hand
that was yellow
and red and blue
as you strolled on the opposite
page from Snow White.

— There were windmills inside
the ball — she said
all running backwards
the yarn had spent itself
by the third turn of the river
by the gingerbread house

still I needed more
I used up my sandal straps
my belt
the ribbon that held my braid

and my hair all of it

finally my veins
weaving them together temporarily
with willow wands and moss

they unravelled too the thread
was all gone
expended extraneous irrelevant
the reel finished
like an aria snipped in two —

Goose-girl
now I remember
you came at last to the end
the secret crease
in the palm of your hand
that led to your heart it ended there

Everyone heard it break
and was sorry

and followed you crying aloud for magic.

RUTH AND NAOMI

Ruth and Naomi
stood in our childhood
rather like nuns in black and white
over the piano
where we practiced duets
my sister and I

— Entreat me not to leave thee —
O gentle Ruth
O excellent Naomi
we loved their misery

Time came in and out again
flax bushes crackled
peach-flavored suns
bubbled the paper on the wall
faded the rug

Nectarines fell a willow died

— I wish you wouldn't leave me —
my sister said and once
(and only once) I beg you not to go

WINDOWPANES

I wrote you on a windowpane
once
at eye level
before the laurels strangled
and the spiders came
centipedes with reddish feet
cobwebs   ravens

open the window for me now
with your long dead hand
the fog is full of fury
and night is just beginning

I wrote you on a windowpane
at my eye's level
my face reflected fully
over your written name
my fingers full of fantasy
feathers   God

SALT WATER

Sometimes the water cracks like ice and
I can see the river
the steamer taking us homeward
rolling a little twisting

nothing travelling inward goes in a straight line

At the river-mouth the joining we
left the Waitemata
waves filed under each other like mutinies
subdued
branches met above absently laving
the deck with fresh-water willows

It was always twilight where the salt water ended

Dark for the rest of the journey
the river boat coughing
its night lamp swinging yellow under the stars
while the river narrowed slowly
devious deliberate
drawing us inward onward with
our noisy chunky probing

Someone singing a lullaby

Animals woke acknowledging our
frail inserted journey
their eyes beaming closer
concealed in their own breathing
banked into fields of clover and fur and early dew

33

I was held in a blanket of many rainbow
colors
like the robe that Joseph wore
the one he was betrayed in

They say I cannot remember
the journey up the river before they put the roads in

but my eyes have the turning habit
and understand removal
I reach for the rail in the early dusk
the rail and the silt and river-smell

where the captain hung his lantern out
and the salt water ended

IN THE ALHAMBRAH ONE GOES SLIGHTLY MAD

Afternoon
Siesta time
I grew anxious and ill in the almond sun
— There were waterfalls — I said
Under the cypress trees I listened
all through
the gardens of pleasure and delight
stammering I searched
gypsy-hearted suffering
memory runs as deep as an idiot's dream

— They were gutters — You were polite
and bored — there had been rain —
I could not remember
we looked and listened
found only roses
because it was autumn chrysanthemums
a fountain or two
and poplars pointing away from Granada
like Arab banners
burning uneven
stoked with the nervous fuel of Spain
You sat on a curving bench
and spoke of home

So I took your hand and we
went away
by the amber walls and the lemon trees
and the quiet pools   I was
listening all the time for waterfalls

SCRIPT IN BAMBOO — INDO-CHINA

Unreasonable write these grasses
fingering
and angular and alien communication
with the dead

uneven lines that speak
uneasily
in watered ink and blood
of multitudes
in the thin lands

And treasonable sing the happy
crickets in the ditch
in the slimy silence
the deafening dismay

All through the night
the grasses write a scribbling
here and there
of warning hands

Speaking of war in the thin lands

TRANSPLANTATION IN A SILVER FRAME

They brought me my dead mother last night
and I became her
my dressing-table filling slowly
with her silver brushes
photographs a fan
jars mysterious and glowing
a silver-handled mirror shabby now

When I picked it up it felt soft
warm
as though with recent fever

It showed dark eyes pale skin black hair
my mother's face not mine

Her gaze as always went beyond me
I laid the mirror down
my hand is suntanned capable my
face rejected hers
as in an unsuccessful graft
where the patient might have died

I went back to bed and wept
— No use Mother pouring this
essence into me   It never was —

I am transparent too   Who then is ghost

My daughter stands beside me now
— Mother why do you cry
what have I done to make you cry —

A LITTLE SALT

(A Little Search)

Whoever knew what
the holy grail resembled a
waterlily or a
rusted can or
the hull of a great big beautiful bomb

or a battleship at anchor

she would not have recognized one
had she found it
panting at her feet waiting
to be captured
for a museum

or if she fell into one head first
it was that kind of a mystery

she was reaching down for
the first ingredient to make
one for herself the waterlily

she was told it had magic properties
and would not bruise when handled

whoever heard of a black and blue chalice

not me she said leaning over
the water
which was full of demons and spirits
screaming curses at
each other all night

if she found the waterlily she
would hold it to the moon
fill it
with white dreams earth-fire
night-ice champagne and
old sins for ballast

as the recipe said tears too

a little salt in every dish her
mother often told her

but of course they all lied

the waterlily bruised badly
showed marks like a cheap suit
the earth-fire
went out puff like a wet candle

the salt dried and blew away

the dreams were the worst of all
when the sun
went down they turned into werewolves

KING AND COUNTRY

She took them from her rosewood box
every afternoon
they lay upon her lap like holy relics

My grandmother seemed very old to me

— And what is posthumous — I asked
— It means that they were dead
both killed in action and the
war was nearly over
the goverment sent these to me
afterwards —

She always wore black

Windows open to the scent of
nectarines and roses
the medals chinking as she handled them
their ribbons glowed
like rainbows on her lap

— Let me hold one please — No —

My grandmother seemed very old to me

CLOUD POEM

Nothing endures
the streets have gone home
small in their narrow stitches
they have worked their way out of my sight

Nothing lasts
snow is hours away
bedded down on a mountain-top
clouds elbow their way towards me
in angry little puffs

They have no wings and no authority
they will not last
flocks without shepherds and the sky
full of whitening wolves

At the high window
I am assailed by miracles
parts and numbers
question-marks flannel my mouth
my face in reflection
wavers like a crooked wedding veil

A broken child appears
a fading wishbone
a pair of huge lovers leaning sideways
a royal bed
with twenty gold posts
and three legs
an angel with a rosy sword
The sky is host to murderers and jets
steel and scavengers
with greasy wings and greedy eyes

Ice on the windowledge begins to melt
the angel rises
flaying the fading wishbone
with rakish sword
the child mends himself and swims away

Only the lovers remain
larger than before they right themselves
fly straight and slow towards me
they paper up my windowpane
with vapor-bones and gentle hands

Their heads fall off their feet dissolve
they drift away dismembered
lonely as tumbleweeds.

APRICOTS

I have found your weakness.
Apricots.
They lie in muzzling moss behind
your every word, fallen
through gold-tipped ravines
in autumn's opulence.

Apricots.
Squashed by the bare brown feet
of children,
nuzzled by tortoises ambling
in forgotten gardens
always in sunlight.

Mine is nectarines.

NIGHT BY THE LAKE

Tin cans turn slowly
settle
again quite soon

Drugged
dissolute
trapped in the lake's non-flowing

Mud and river-things
gathering
an urgent congregation
of dragonflies
demons webbed
in fine membrane

the skin of half-forgotten
cravings

Terror coming silently
as my foot slips
water laps the mark

Shows nothing
I am therefore
by
act of water

                    gone
                    forever

THE GUNS OF ALAMEIN

No-one remains to listen now.
The guns of Alamein fell silent years ago;
people sometimes say, comparing then to now,
your war was worth the cost.
The old refrain wears thin; for me
no war is understood

        no death forgiven.

No-one remains to count them now.
The pale camellias falling
by the hundreds from my father's trees;
nor anyone to call two children home
across a waterfall,
an orchard plump with budding nectarines.

The guns of Alamein.
The desert rising, dragging like an ocean
at the moon's full yolk
took this away.

The memory perspired in silence
poisonous as particles of burning sand
until this day,
when suddenly I see camellias growing tall
and weep.

So far the hills of home,
so permanent your sleep.

CALLOWAY STREET

THE NEWLY—WEDS RETURN

Two strangers
slept
in my house last night

in the same bed

I know one quite
well
who calls me
Mother

The other tries to

VANESSA at 4 a.m.

this life
has no skin

there wasn't time to
organize
the molecules
where shall I find
a robe
a counterpane
a featherbed to warm
this life
that has no skin

if I lay my hand
upon it
somebody will scream

46

JENNIFER

Jennifer used to smile a lot
She had been a radiant bride
a sunny satisfied mother
with her brood. In her suburb
simple-mindedness
bespoke success. Jennifer qualified.

Her house was a haven of comfort
where she smiled and served and smiled
believing in all things good.

Her children left for marriage
or for war or both and Jennifer

Took up sculpture. Now she
descends to her cellar daily
as to the mouth of Hades
goggled and masked for destruction
or creation. Incognito shapeless
she challenges metal with fire
provoking to life a
brand-new generation of faceless people

Unspeakable families
who never smile back.

TWENTY-TWO CALLOWAY STREET

I live
in a house
with a hole in the middle

just like a donut

the ceiling
is high beyond
my reach
the floor drops
suddenly
under my feet

you could hang
yourself
if you had the notion

THE LIBERATION OF MRS. JONES

Men are Okay
I happen to like them
in spite
of several serious defects
which are however
becoming to them

I am speaking in particular
of male chauvinism
I do not think
they should be denied this
small vanity

After all we have ours
don't we
Gloria Betty and all you other Sisters

However
this does not necessarily mean
that I would wish my
daughter to marry one of them . . .

HOBBIES ARE GOOD FOR WOMEN

Bert and Eloise
a fine and stolid pair
he working at finance continuously
no other woman
complicating his life

He has always been faithful

Business his only pleasure
more and more crashing around
the forests of finance
like a moose intent upon a mating call

Loving his Eloise
speaking of her kindly
she was painting now
nice enough stuff not serious
of course but hobbies are
good for women keep them
out of trouble
and the psychiatric wards

Nice for her
and a hell of a lot cheaper for Bert

Mildly proud he showed
her paintings to their friends
thought her content
to blossom in his praise forever

He was wrong

ROADS

(You take the — Road
And I'll take the — Road...)

Correct Change
Only
By-Pass
Business
Exit   Exit   Exit

Innerspring
Sister Sarah
Tells Fortunes   Reads Palms

Exit
to Calloway Street

Stop Welcome Station
Stop Trucks
Weigh yourselves
Don't cheat

Fine of Fifty Dollars
for littering
ExitExit Exit

Please don't sit your
Children on the Counters
By order of the
Health Department

Exit
to Annie's Log Road
Exit to Gas Food
Jones Swamp

Exit Exit Exit

If you love Jesus
Honk!

51

ON THE BEACH

A nun
in her black and white
habit
walking alone on the chill
Wilmington sands

Her knees show
things have certainly changed

The beach goes for miles
the nun marches on
stepping between the spikes
of our window
Catherine walking through the spokes
of her wheel?

Nobody looks at her
as she passes
at her pale virtuous knees.

The sun comes out
and birds hop away from her
as though she carries a broom.

We turn up the heat
have another drink.

THE LADY AT 457

Lacking all else I
have scorn
brilliant cantilevered
splendid wrath

I am indiscriminate
everything bows before my tongue

I tell tales pass judgements
on strangers friends alike

I have no enemies

I bring forth daily
packages and purses of
imagined heresies and sins

and plant them where I wish
in other people's gardens
where they flourish
like forbidden poppies.

ANYONE

Wouldn't you think
after all that
I could sleep

after the turmoil
effort
odyssey

anyone
should be able
to sleep

not lie awake
printed
onto the sheets

staring
at the softening
holes over my head

holes
in the black Swiss cheese
of the night

anyone
should learn
how to forget

POSSESSION

Jane read her magazines
about the dreary middle years
the empty nest
children gone
mother forlorn;

Laughed aloud
showing her pretty teeth.

Said to her lover
one day
"The family nest
is an uncomfortable place
when the children grow up
anyway. I'm glad
mine are gone
I'm not a possessive woman
thank God;
I only wish sometimes I had
authority again."

"Like over me?" he asked
"Perhaps," she said
never saw him again.

SCRAMBLED EGGS

The front burner
is broken
a wire loose somewhere

Like a demented brain
it chugs along on high
nothing else

I burn everything even eggs

Here comes rescue
a man to mend my burner
He wears a beard
loose tennis shoes
looks like Randall Jarrell

He drags the stove
ruthlessly from the wall

Oh God look at the dirt

I flinch
Shame
the least I could do
is keep the kitchen clean

He does not notice
my sloth
concentrates on the stove
wrestles with it
is blind or a gentleman
or both

I watch him repair my front burner

He tells me how to scramble eggs

MR HALSTEAD

When the sons
of the Halstead house
on Calloway Street became
old enough to bring
the girls from St. Elizabeth's
home
Howard Halstead
gave up golf and stayed home more.

He is now an authority
on skirts legs blouses eyes
bosoms dimples
and the academic curriculum
of St. Elizabeth's which
is all the poor kids can

safely discuss with him.

THURSDAY

All night and half of a day
she thought about dying

closing her door willing
death closer with
his cleft tongue and breath
that smelled of cabbages

The air at her bed was
fog The floor sank like
wet sponge There was no rain

She said she had a headache

And by next Thursday it
was all over The sun shone
brittle and brassy outside

Her skin had flaked a little
her voice changed It strained
and cracked
like an adolescent boy's

One of her children came home
they quarrelled

It was high noon   Dry noon
she started to drink again

FRECKLES

That summer
there were two
operations
on Calloway Street

One was a
hysterectomy
the other
a disappointment

Martha-Ann
found age-spots
suddenly etched
on her legs and arms

Bought some
new makeup

Called them freckles

THE DRUGSTORE

It is lit but uninviting
sterile glass plastered with
gaudy posters
tiredly attached
with scotch tape

a notice for church bazaar
a ball game picture
of a young man running for office
somewhere
ambitious clean-cut young rooster

(no-one could be as honest
and upstanding as he looks)

icecream sundaes cosmetics
candies coke shall we go in
sit at a peeling plastic counter
pleasure ourselves
with coffee smoke
staring the while at a cabinet
afloat
with accoutrements of modern life
sex to medi-care
ex-lax aspirin
sleeping pills an enema display
a white bedpan
hanging by its throat

we stand hesitate
while pills bottled and anonymous
a pair of truculent rubber gloves
a magazine
with pictures of film stars and their
illicit loves
the young politician
the bedpan
and three late customers all stare out
through the lumatic glass

it's late we pass

1826 CALLOWAY STREET

Jane was
all heart warmth intuition
feeling
no brain

she said
to her lover one day
(a new one and handsome)
— I understand
you perfectly —

he put on his clothes
and left
nobody likes
to be understood quite that much.

ANTONIA WHO RAN AWAY

I am Antonia
and I never was really lost

I have been here
in this garble of truthful stars
treading water
over the seasons weaving
waiting
till somebody calls me home
lovingly
by my name
reeling me in hand over hand
gently
by the strands of my long long hair

calling my name
patiently
over and over again

Antonia   Antonia   Antonia

THE CALLOWAY STREET KIDS GO TO THE NEW NIGHTSPOT

Black as coal shiny
aggressive
Sings like an angel
Alley cat strayed south on
skinny legs
Big voice, Microphone a club

Needling, cradling notes
— rednecks whitenecks college kids
down here slummin' it
you should have known better —

Sings like an angel Everyone polite
mesmerized
by snaky black dress flickering legs
white teeth big teeth
Walking singing stalking under
the spotlight, under the nerves

A stray come home again
singing loud in the dark room

THE EXODUS

Our children grew
giraffe necks
split hooves forked
tongues
elephant ears and wings

flew away rejoicing

The house groans
like an empty stomach
punishing itself in
windy syllables
day and night

nights are the worst

we have no friends old
or new suddenly
no servants either

they are uppity and
hard to keep these days

so are friends

THE SCIENCE

OF

SMALL THINGS

Knowing content
is to invite
devils
to take it away

I had not
spoken
yet they came
they were delighted

I
am victimized
by
violets

I must have
said a name
aloud
in my sleep

Impertinence
of
cobwebs
in my favorite
tree

Irrelevant
anatomy
of rainbows
Half of an ellipse
is half
of a manacle
and not
the sum of anything
that balances

Because
you find I can weep
at last
does not mean
I could not
have done it before

NOTES AT A GALLERY

Nobody more alone than the poet
the reading over
finished and the room quiet

the smell of betrayal

he stands like an egg without a shell
contained in membrane
what does he say now

where does he go

THE DEVIL

The Devil
is always young
and hard to catch

I try all the time
but he moves fast
for someone

denied forever
the use
of his angel wings

FISHER – GIRL POEM

Poet
I do not like
much that you write

but this one
though
ordinary enough
strikes
at my throat
my veins go limp

my voice goes
out
little jewels

the size of
orange-pips
clang in my head

I am
a fisher-girl
naked

alone on
her prow
flying her net

in a sea bright with lovers

STIRRING A POEM

I find no comfort
in my poetry.

What made you think I did?

Stirring
the bread of it
the yeasty taste sickens:
kneading the dough
brings me to no conclusion.

I am astonished sometimes
at its verbiage
its disobedience.

It is a poultice
laden with inconsistencies.

I should go to church more often.

WHISTLING

Yesterday
        yesterday
came like a whistle
        long
in the middle
        loose
at the end
In the beginning
        brash
and beguiling
        shaking the tears
from a dropsical sky

Somebody said
        "I never could whistle!"
Neither could I
        neither could I

TWENTY HORSES

I was not strong at all
                just competent
and young
You never knew the difference
pushing me out into the never amiable night
                where animals yapped
                from strange places
and one never knew

if they were wolves or not

I went
and grew as strong as twenty horses
twenty horses strong
                cunning
                and surefooted
as the white unicorn in the mythical wood

I change my skin often
I can stand alone for hours
                listening

MARIGOLDS

My mother dipped me in a rainbow
I nearly drowned

flowers spoke in colors to me
shouted out my sense
they say

and the blue Pacific
brought me gifts
blossoms and fallen branches
once a visitation
of illicit gold

I nearly died with joy

Don't bring me eucalyptus now
or quiet deadened flowers
for my table

there is finality in dried bouquets
and I would rather
breathe in joy

a gold coin in my hand
and marigolds to lie on

WATER

There is not enough
water
to drift in
to drown in

water
dissolves so fast
sinking
out of time

and words
are wishes
tucked in the lining
of shoes

like mad money

KINDLING WOOD

A witch
who brings
her own matches
to the fire

is well worth the burning

WATERSOUNDS

We are all
joined to each other by wires
and the world
is full of water

We stumble upon
coral
sea-anemones
our hands holding
the wires
tightening overhead
white fingers tugging

Strands of our hair
stiffen
and sing humming
like smoke

We move slowly
nourished
by water
joined to each other
forever
in waterlilies and weeds

NIGHTINGALES

No birds
should be singing now
unless
they are nightingales

Unless
they are nightingales
and sing
for the last time

POETS AND PROPHETS

Picture it
the rock that was all grey
but known to spout

fountains
of life-giving water
when struck

at the right time
and hard
by a particular

prophet using they say
an ordinary
stick or walking-cane

now
brothers and sisters
we must seek water

in other places
this rock yields metaphor
instead

and urchins speaking
roughly
with cracked voices

parched lips
stones litter the desert
profanely

melt in their blue
faces
the prophet snores

in the shadow of buzzards.

WATERCOLORS

Red moss
flowing
under the waterfall

tree ferns
turning silver
in the slight wind

long grass
weeping
into my child's hands
like the hair

of wild angels

FRECKLES AND A RED DOG

The little boy
whose ears stick out
walks home from school so close

Hello there
I had one like you

Another boy with merry eyes
missing tooth
freckles
rolls in the autumn leaves
with a red dog

Hello Boy — Hello Dog
I had both of you once

From my meager porch
on the street
where the windows walk
I try for words
making sounds
that stick in the peeling paint.

Hello Boy — Goodbye Freckles
Big Ears — Shiny dog.

I stir my November heart
like a witch
with an old ladle . . .

CARYATID REMOVED

I am standing here in the sun
where the south begins

but the rain has gone right through me

my bones understand it all
the water coming hard cold as the track of lizards

as the touching of blind fish

and my marble dress releasing it slowly

I have had so much of water
I could be

my own baptismal font
marble hands cupped to hold the round shape

of it secure

for the sweep of clerical lace
the infant's pure howling

A READING OF THE SUMMER TREES

The trees of summer afternoons in France.
Museum trees that hang in gilded frames
through white-walled Sunday visits.

Today I brought them home behind my eyes
as undetected emeralds in the ore
their centuries intact, their leaves
a gypsy's reading in a teacup.

They ring me now, my dark-heart trees
Carolina oaks, their wordlessness
a constant talking, painful as obituaries,
                    asserting deep authority
blurting fireflies against a newlit window.

A pair of mockingbirds is shaken loose.
The sky keeps noble distance and is quiet;
silence balances self. I read the leaves,
a gypsy, fortuneteller, queen.

I read on and on, my fingers to the sap;
I find words. I come out even.